BEI GRIN MACHT SICH IHR WISSEN BEZAHLT

- Wir veröffentlichen Ihre Hausarbeit, Bachelor- und Masterarbeit

- Ihr eigenes eBook und Buch - weltweit in allen wichtigen Shops

- Verdienen Sie an jedem Verkauf

Jetzt bei www.GRIN.com hochladen und kostenlos publizieren

Burkhard Werner

Mark Twain's Theory of the Humorous Story and "The Notorious Jumping Frog of Calaveras County"

GRIN Verlag

Bibliografische Information der Deutschen Nationalbibliothek:

Die Deutsche Bibliothek verzeichnet diese Publikation in der Deutschen Nationalbibliografie; detaillierte bibliografische Daten sind im Internet über http://dnb.d-nb.de/ abrufbar.

Dieses Werk sowie alle darin enthaltenen einzelnen Beiträge und Abbildungen sind urheberrechtlich geschützt. Jede Verwertung, die nicht ausdrücklich vom Urheberrechtsschutz zugelassen ist, bedarf der vorherigen Zustimmung des Verlages. Das gilt insbesondere für Vervielfältigungen, Bearbeitungen, Übersetzungen, Mikroverfilmungen, Auswertungen durch Datenbanken und für die Einspeicherung und Verarbeitung in elektronische Systeme. Alle Rechte, auch die des auszugsweisen Nachdrucks, der fotomechanischen Wiedergabe (einschließlich Mikrokopie) sowie der Auswertung durch Datenbanken oder ähnliche Einrichtungen, vorbehalten.

Impressum:

Copyright © 2003 GRIN Verlag GmbH
Druck und Bindung: Books on Demand GmbH, Norderstedt Germany
ISBN: 978-3-656-16647-4

Dieses Buch bei GRIN:

http://www.grin.com/de/e-book/191702/mark-twain-s-theory-of-the-humorous-story-and-the-notorious-jumping

GRIN - Your knowledge has value

Der GRIN Verlag publiziert seit 1998 wissenschaftliche Arbeiten von Studenten, Hochschullehrern und anderen Akademikern als eBook und gedrucktes Buch. Die Verlagswebsite www.grin.com ist die ideale Plattform zur Veröffentlichung von Hausarbeiten, Abschlussarbeiten, wissenschaftlichen Aufsätzen, Dissertationen und Fachbüchern.

Besuchen Sie uns im Internet:

http://www.grin.com/

http://www.facebook.com/grincom

http://www.twitter.com/grin_com

Bayerische Julius-Maximilians-Universität
Würzburg

Institut für Anglistik und Amerikanistik

Wintersemester 2002/2003
Proseminar Englische Literaturwissenschaft:
American Realism and Local Color

Seminararbeit

Thema:
Mark Twain's Theory of the Humorous Story
and
"The Notorious Jumping Frog of Calaveras County"

Verfasser:
Burkhard Werner

Table of contents

I. Introduction …………………………………………………………….3

II. Short Biography of Mark Twain …………………………………………3

III. The History of "The Jumping Frog" …………………….…...…..……4

IV. The Structure of "The Jumping Frog" ……………..……………...…..4

V. The Theory of the Humorous Story ……………………………………..6

VI. Elements of the Humorous Story in "The Jumping Frog" ……..…….7

VII. Final Conclusion …………………………………………………….....9

VIII. Bibliography ……………………………………………………….10

Counted Words: 2802

I. Introduction

Today Mark Twain or using his real name Samuel Langhorne Clemens is often seen as one of the most important authors of the American Realism. His Theory of the Humorous Story is one of the most important theories of writing a funny story.

Those are the questions to be answered. Based on interpretations of one of his most famous stories "The Notorious Jumping Frog of Calaveras County", Twain intensions will be shown. This means there will be shown what influenced Twain in his writings and which different interpretations of his works, in this case exemplary of "The Notorious Jumping Frog of Calaveras County", are possible. In the end there will have to be considered if the "The Notorious Jumping Frog of Calaveras County" is really a humorous story in sense of Twain's Theory of the Humorous Story or not.

II. Short Biography of Mark Twain

Samuel Clemens was born on November 30th in the year 1835 in the village Florida in the state Missouri. He grew up in a town called Hannibal. There he received little formal education. In the year 1847 his father died and he had to support the family. So he worked for his brother Orion who became a publisher. In the year 1853 Mark Twain began a three-year travel period in which he went to St. Louis, New York and Philadelphia. In 1864 he started ti write for the *Californian* During the next years he established some important friendships with the writer Bret Harte and the professional lecturer Artemus Ward[1]. In 1865 Mark Twain published his first popular story "The Notorious Jumping Frog of Calaveras County". In 1870 he married Olivia Landon and moved to Hartford in the state Connecticut. In 1876 Mark Twain published

---

[1] Artemus Ward was the pseudonym of Charles Farrar Browne.

"The Adventures of Tom Sawyer" and in 1882 "The Prince and the Pauper". In the year 1884 his most famous work "The Adventures of Huckleberry Finn" was published. In 1904 Twain's wife died two years after two of his daughters had died. Because of these terrible circumstances Twain lost his optimistic tone in writing and wrote more somber works like "What is Man" in 1906 or "The Mysterious Stranger" which was published in 1916, six years after Twains death on April 21st 1910.

III. The History of "The Jumping Frog"

On 4th December 1864 Mark Twain traveled to Calaveras County in California. He stayed there until he went back to San Francisco on the 25th February 1865. There he spent very much time in a bar at Angel's Camp. In this bar Twain met Ben Coon, who told him the story of the jumping frog. Twain liked the story and made an entry in his notebook. Back in San Francisco was asked by his friend Artemus Ward to write a short story for a volume of humorous sketches. Twain wanted to use his entry of this notebook to write a story about the jumping frog. Although he finished his writing too late for the inclusion in Ward's sketch-volume. "The Notorious Jumping Frog of Calaveras County", often also "The Celebrated Jumping Frog of Calaveras County" called, was first published in the *New York Saturday Press* on the 18th November 1865. Then it was again published in Twain's first book of short stories "The Celebrated Jumping Frog of Calaveras County, and Other Sketches" in April 1867. First it was not very successful. In America it really didn't sell well, but the there were big sales in the United Kingdom.

IV. The structure of "The Jumping Frog"

The story plays in the mining camp of Angel's in Calaveras County in California. "The Jumping Frog" consists of one frame story with three stories within. The protagonist of the story is the "I"-narrator "[...] who can be identified with the fictional persona "Mark Twain"."[2]

The frame story starts with the search for Reverend Leonidas W. Smiley. Therefore the "I"-narrator contacts Simon Wheeler. Mr. Wheeler does not know Leonidas Smiley, but he knows a person called Jim Smiley. Wheeler forces the "I"-narrator to listen the stories about Jim Smiley.

The first story is about Jim Smiley's horse, "the fifteen-minute nag"[3], which he uses to win money in horse races. This horse always wins even after having bad starts.

The second story is about Jim's fighting "little small bull-pup"[4] called Andrew Jackson.[5] This dog also never loses in a fight. The dog has a special trick. It pretends the loser and then uses a special bite to win. However one day Andrew Jackson is betrayed by Jim Smiley. The dog cannot use that bite and dies of sadness.

The third story is the story about the frog. The story does not start with the description of the animal and the bets, but with the catching and the training of the frog, called Daniel Webster.[6] Smiley is convinced that the frog can out jump any frog of Calaveras County. One day he bets with a stranger for 50$. However the stranger has no frog and Smiley is going way to get one. While Jim is getting a frog the stranger fills the frog up with quail shot. Because of this the frog cannot jump anymore and so the untrained frog of the stranger wins the contest.

After this last story the frame story is picked up again. There Simon Wheeler is being called from outside. So the narrator can escape before Simon Wheeler can start his next story about Jim Smiley's one-eyed cow without a tail.

---

[2] Messent, Peter. *The Short Works of Mark Twain: A Critical Study.* Philadelphia: Pennsylvania UP, 2001. 26.
[3] Clemens, Samuel Langhorne. "The Notorious Jumping Frog of Calaveras County." *The Norton Anthology of American Literature.* 2Bde. Ed. Nina Baym et al. New York: Norton, ³1989. 2. 22.
[4] Clemens, Samuel Langhorne. "The Notorious Jumping Frog of Calaveras County." *The Norton Anthology of American Literature.* 2Bde. Ed. Nina Baym et al. New York: Norton, ³1989. 2. 22.
[5] Andrew Jackson was in the Battle of New Orleans General of the American troops. After that he was a democratic President of the United States form 1829 to 1837.
[6] Daniel Webster was an republican senator from 1827 to 1841.

V. The Theory of the Humorous Story

Mark Twain in the year 1897 published the Theory of the Humorous Story. It was published as "How to Tell a Story and Other Essays". There Mark Twain shows how you should write a funny story.

There Mark Twain says that, he does not claim that he could tell a story as it should be told, he only claims that he knows how a story should be told. He also says, that "The humorous story is American, the comic story is English, the witty story is French."[7] The humorous story is a work of art. There are also many types of stories, but the humorous is the most difficult kind of. The art of telling a humorous story was created in America and stayed there. The effect of the humorous story lies upon the manner of the telling, the effect of the comic and witty story upon the matter of the telling. "The humorous story is how you tell it, and the comic story is what you tell about."[8] The humorous story also "finishes with a nub, point, snapper, or whatever you like to call it."[9] There you have to listen very carefully to the story to understand the nub. In European literature the nub is known from the beginning on and there is no attention necessary. In humorous stories you have to find the humor on your own.

You should write about something you know many facts about. You should also use good grammar when you are writing. A good story shall accomplish something and arrive somewhere, but the writer shall not follow a purpose. The story should also be long and detailed. Then the episodes of a tale shall be necessary parts of the tale and shall help to develop it. However you should use pauses in the story to get an unexpected ending. The characters in the story shall also be clearly defined. You should also use the right word and not a

---

[7] Clemens, Samuel Langhorne. "How to Tell a Story." *The Norton Anthology of American Literature*. 2Bde. Ed. Nina Baym et al. New York: Norton, ³1989. 2.218.
[8] Siesing, Gina M. *DIWE InterChange on Samuel Clemens' (aka Mark Twain's) "How to Tell a Story" and "The Notorious Jumping Frog of Calaveras County"*. 16 October 1996. 12 February 2003. < http://www.cwrl.utexas.edu/~gsiesing/316/interchanges/twain.html>.
[9] Clemens, Samuel Langhorne. "How to Tell a Story." *The Norton Anthology of American Literature*. 2Bde. Ed. Nina Baym et al. New York: Norton, ³1989. 2.218.

synonym, which has not the exact meaning. The style you have to use should be simple and straightforward.

VI. Elements of the Humorous Story in "The Jumping Frog"

Mark Twain knows many things about the story he writes of. Like shown above, the story about the real Jim Smiley was told to him when he visited Angel's Camp in Calaveras County.

The characters of the story are also clear defined. The frame teller of the story seems to be well educated. He looks down on the typical westerner, like to Simon Wheeler. The exaggerated formal way of describing makes him humorless and makes the reader antipathy toward him.

Simon Wheeler is modeled on Ben Coon who told Mark Twain the frog story. He is a good-natured old man who is so focused on the telling of the story that he does not forget any detail.

Jim Smiley is the frog trainer, horse and dog better who bets on really everything. He seems to be a simple-minded man.

One important element of the Humorous Story is Simon Wheeler's way of telling s story is the development into a literary form of humor. Twain shows this also in "How to Tell a Story":

> To string incongruities and absurdities together in a wandering and sometimes purposeless way, and seem innocently unaware that they are absurdities, is the basis of the American art, if my position is correct. Another feature is the slurring of the point. A third is the dropping of a studied remark apparently without knowing it, as if one where thinking aloud. The fourth and last is the pause.[10]

All these techniques are devices of indirection and also techniques of betting at poker. For example the pauses are to surprise the reader with another clue.

---

[10] Clemens, Samuel Langhorne. "How to Tell a Story." *The Norton Anthology of American Literature.* 2Bde. Ed. Nina Baym et al. New York: Norton, ³1989. 2. 220.

In poker it is the same. You make pauses for bluffing the other players. For instance a "bust"[11] hand means that the player has a straight flush.[12]

Another part of humor is also Simon Wheeler's apparent failure to discriminate between the real and the fabulous. Or between the important and the trivial is the chief source of humor.[13]

There is also the influence of comic force. There is an "unwitting collaboration between the two narrators."[14] The "I"-narrator uses Standard English and it seems that he is educated. Simon Wheeler on the opposite uses very often dialect and is more like a typical westerner. The "I"-narrator seems to be form the West, but has lived in the East. He also seems very arrogant. Simon Wheeler is more natural, but he is always talking and annoying.

There is also "the impossibility of being sure of Wheeler's deadpan".[15] "Twain comments that the purveyor of a humorous story must act or even believe that the story he is telling concerns a grave matter to which no humor is attributable."[16] Twain describes Wheeler as regarding his story with earnestness and sincerity and telling in monotonous tone. So the character of Wheeler is very important to show that Twain is using his "Theory of the Humorous Story" in "The Jumping Frog". Also "style and structure [serve] as a masterpiece of Twain".[17] These are essential for the humor of the sketch.[18]

What is also important is that he uses dialect in "The Jumping Frog". Words like "I'll resk forty dollars"[19] or "feller"[20] show that the author should write in

---

[11] Clemens, Samuel Langhorne. "The Notorious Jumping Frog of Calaveras County." *The Norton Anthology of American Literature*. 2Bde. Ed. Nina Baym et al. New York: Norton, ³1989. 2. 22.

[12] Covici Jr., Pascal. *Mark Twain's Humor*. Dallas: Southern Methodist UP, 1967. 49.

[13] Cox, James M. *Mark Twain: The Fate of Humor*. Princeton: Princeton UP, 1966. 29.

[14] Cox, James M. *Mark Twain: The Fate of Humor*. Princeton: Princeton UP, 1966. 29.

[15] Cox, James M. *Mark Twain: The Fate of Humor*. Princeton: Princeton UP, 1966. 29.

[16] Siesing, Gina M. *DIWE InterChange on Samuel Clemens' (aka Mark Twain's) "How to Tell a Story" and "The Notorious Jumping Frog of Calaveras County"*. 16 October 1996. 12 February 2003. < http://www.cwrl.utexas.edu/~gsiesing/316/interchanges/twain.html>.

[17] Cox, James M. *Mark Twain: The Fate of Humor*. Princeton: Princeton UP, 1966. 29.

[18] Cox, James M. *Mark Twain: The Fate of Humor*. Princeton: Princeton UP, 1966. 29.

[19] Clemens, Samuel Langhorne. "The Notorious Jumping Frog of Calaveras County." *The Norton Anthology of American Literature*. 2Bde. Ed. Nina Baym et al. New York: Norton, ³1989. 2. 24.

[20] Clemens, Samuel Langhorne. "The Notorious Jumping Frog of Calaveras County." *The Norton Anthology of American Literature*. 2Bde. Ed. Nina Baym et al. New York: Norton, ³1989. 2. 21.

his own word and his dialect. This is one of Twain's attitudes toward the writing of a good story.

The "nub" of the story is without any doubt the repetition the earlier phrase of the stranger: "I don't see no p'ints about that frog that's any better'n any other frog."[21] This is the exploitation of Smiley's own innocence.

The story itself is also not very funny. The three tales of Wheeler have not many humorous parts. So the matter of telling is not funny. The manner of telling is very funny. The endless telling of Simon Wheeler and the impossibility of the narrator to escape and also the language make "The Jumping Frog" very humorous.

The story is long and detailed written. The tales within the tale are necessary parts of the whole story. They help to develop the story. The figure of Jim Smiley is introduced and characterized. The other characters are characterized by the description of "I"-narrator as shown before.

VII. Final Conclusion

"The Notorious Jumping Frog of Calaveras County" is a masterpiece of Mark Twain's writing after his Theory of the Humorous Story. As shown this story is a humorous story in Twain's sense of writing a humorous story. Mark Twain uses almost all of the criteria of the theory in this. Although this theory was created after the writing of "The Jumping Frog" in the year 1897. "The Notorious Jumping Frog of Calaveras County" was Twain's first popular story and it has nearly all important elements of the humorous story. However this story was not the first and only humorous story of Mark Twain. There were many stories that followed.

---

[21] Clemens, Samuel Langhorne. "The Notorious Jumping Frog of Calaveras County." *The Norton Anthology of American Literature*. 2Bde. Ed. Nina Baym et al. New York: Norton, [3]1989. 2. 24.

VIII. Bibliography

Texts:

Clemens, Samuel Langhorne. "How to Tell a Story." *The Norton Anthology of American Literature.* 2Bde. Ed. Nina Baym et al. New York: Norton, ³1989. 2. 220.

Clemens, Samuel Langhorne. "The Notorious Jumping Frog of Calaveras County." *The Norton Anthology of American Literature.* 2Bde. Ed. Nina Baym et al. New York: Norton, ³1989. 2.

Literature:

Covici Jr., Pascal. *Mark Twain's Humor.* Dallas: Southern Methodist UP, 1967.

Cox, James M. *Mark Twain: The Fate of Humor.* Princeton: Princeton UP, 1966.

Messent, Peter. *The Short Works of Mark Twain: A Critical Study.* Philadelphia: Pennsylvania UP, 2001.

Lynn, Kenneth S. *Mark Twain and Southwestern Humor.* Boston/Toronto: Atlantic Monthly Press, 1959.

Sloane, David E.E. *Student Companion to Mark Twain.* Westport: Greenwood Press, 2001.

Wilson, James D. *A reader's guide to the short stories of Mark Twain.* Boston: Hall. 1987.

Internet Resources:

Siesing, Gina M. *DIWE InterChange on Samuel Clemens' (aka Mark Twain's) "How to Tell a Story" and "The Notorious Jumping Frog of Calaveras County".* 16 October 1996. 12 February 2003. < http://www.cwrl.utexas.edu/~gsiesing/316/interchanges/twain.html>.